S0-AEX-546

Visitation of the
Holy Spirit

Visitation of the Holy Spirit

by
Dennis Burke

HARRISON HOUSE
Tulsa Oklahoma

Unless otherwise indicated, all Scripture quotations are taken from the *King James Version* of the Bible.

2nd Printing

Visitation of the Holy Spirit
ISBN 0-89274-468-5
Copyright © 1987 by Dennis Burke
P. O. Box 793
Arlington, Texas 76010

Published by Harrison House, Inc.
P. O. Box 35035
Tulsa, Oklahoma 74153

Contents

1
Visitation of the Holy Spirit

During the ministry of Jesus, the city of Jerusalem was experiencing a struggle. There was a spiritual battle going on between the religious ideas the people had become comfortable with and the demands of God's powerful presence.

The words of Jesus penetrated the people with clear principles of God's Kingdom. Preaching frequently in the city and the temple, He presented the power of God to heal and deliver; and the multitudes hearing Him were set free. Yet those who should have been most eager to hear the Gospel refused to accept God in their midst.

Coming down the Mount of Olives on a colt, Jesus approached the city that God called "the City of Peace," Jerusalem. The people began to rejoice and shout praises to God for the mighty works they had seen. In an overwhelming demonstration of adulation, they laid their garments and palm branches in the pathway before Him. He received their praise as King, Possessor of heaven and earth, which He deserved. It was time to recognize that heaven's royalty had come.

Amid this tremendous display, it became clear that Jerusalem as a whole had divided loyalties. They had learned to live religiously content without God. Their comfort and complacency blinded their eyes to what belonged to them.

Jesus looked upon the city of God's people and began to weep because they had missed the season of God's visitation in the flesh. Jesus was God's mercy, peace, and power made available to them.

And when he was come near, he beheld the city, and wept over it,

8

Saying, If thou hadst known, even thou, at least in this thy day, the things which belong unto thy peace! but now they are hid from thine eyes.

For the days shall come upon thee, that thine enemies shall cast a trench about thee, and compass thee round, and keep thee in on every side,

And shall lay thee even with the ground, and thy children within thee; and they shall not leave in thee one stone upon another; because thou knewest not the time of thy visitation.

Luke 19:41-44

The very ones who should have known the Messiah could not recognize God standing in their midst. They missed the coming of the Holy Spirit and the birthing of the Church. Instead of embracing the Messiah, they rejected Him.

By rejecting God's visitation, the Israelites set into motion their own destruction. Jesus declared prophetically what the result of their calloused hearts would be. (vv. 43,44.) He foretold with pinpoint accuracy the events that would befall them.

In less than forty years the Romans besieged the city, cast a trench about it, and kept its inhabitants in on every side. Titus built a wall surrounding the city and cut off all hope of escape. He commanded his soldiers to "dig up the city," so the entire city was leveled. It would be nearly 1900 years before the people would again pray at the Wailing Wall where Jesus had stood.

What was true of God's city in those days can be true of His people today. There is a fresh breath of the Holy Spirit being breathed into the Body of Christ. As the Holy Spirit reaches out, welcome Him and embrace His ways with a willing heart. Sense His promptings and be quick to respond. Hear His voice and do not hesitate to obey.

In the beginning when that breath of God began pulsating through Adam's cold, lifeless body, he was made alive. A vibrant relationship developed, and

Adam walked in unbroken fellowship with God.

As God breathes on His people today, He pulls us into a deeper relationship — a dimension in Him that is untouched by human efforts or ambitions. Only those who yield in willing obedience can experience this updraft of the Holy Spirit.

Today is a time of visitation! The Holy Spirit is moving in the Church to restore His power. This restoration is the Holy Spirit in a manifest and resident manner.

We dare not take lightly this sense of God's presence reaching out to lift us, or we will be left behind as He moves forward with His plan. Like Jerusalem then, many in His nation (the Church) today have pulled back from the moving of the Spirit.

If you miss the time of the Holy Spirit's visitation, you will set into motion your own ruin. If you do not reach up to Him to walk in those things which belong to you, and in those things He will reveal to you, your spiritual sight will grow dim.

Satan will dig a trench around you until it looks like there is no way out. He will keep you in on every side and lay you even with the ground. What you set your hand to do will not be blessed by God. You will have to rely on manipulation rather than the manifestation of the Holy Spirit.

Sadly, for many believers, God is no more real than He is to the unbeliever. God hasn't left them; but if they do not walk toward the light, they will be drawing back from Him.

Change can seem so difficult. The light of the Holy Spirit continually points you to new territory, at least new to you. The unknown can seem uncomfortable. You may not feel as secure in new surroundings. Even new spiritual revelation can be unsettling to your mind.

If you draw back from His dealings or direction, you pull away from His light. Soon the dimming light gives way to darkness. The dimension He was drawing you into is hidden from your eyes in the darkness of disobedience. You can almost hear the sound of trenches being dug around you. Though you cry out for victory, there is none in disobedience. *Victory exists only when you obey.*

Job cried out to God in his time of distress. Let's read it:

> **My soul is weary of my life; I will leave my complaint upon myself; I will speak in the bitterness of my soul.**
>
> **I will say unto God, Do not condemn me; shew me wherefore thou contendest with me.**
>
> **Job 10:1,2**

Job, feeling as if he were at the end, said to God, "Show me where I have left the path You want me on."

If you come to God in total openness and honesty, He will not condemn you. Instead He will breathe afresh in your spirit and ignite you with His power. Later Job said, **Thou hast granted me life and favour, and thy visitation hath preserved my spirit** (v. 12).

A fresh, personal visitation of the Holy Spirit is the only way to remain in

13

the stream of God's vision. In every fresh move of the Holy Spirit there are those God uses in great ways to ignite people. They are motivated by the vision of His sweeping power.

In Acts, chapter 10, we find one of the most significant events of the early Church. It opened an entirely new dimension of God's redemption.

> There was a certain man in Caesarea called Cornelius, a centurion of the band called the Italian band,
>
> A devout man, and one that feared God with all his house, which gave much alms to the people, and prayed to God alway.
>
> He saw in a vision evidently about the ninth hour of the day an angel of God coming in to him, and saying unto him, Cornelius.
>
> And when he looked on him, he was afraid, and said, What is it, Lord? And he said unto him, Thy prayers and thine alms are come up for a memorial before God.

Acts 10:1-4

Cornelius was a Gentile — a man without a covenant — who had a deep hunger for God. This hunger was expressed two ways in his life: he gave alms and he prayed.

There is a deep spiritual connection between giving, praying, and a fresh moving of the Holy Spirit. God looks for those who pray and give. The significance of these two areas is that one reaches into the spiritual realm and the other into the material realm.

Through prayer, the channels of the Spirit can open to release God's anointing. Through giving, our willingness to obey links spiritual power with the material need of our lives. God honors our giving. Our acts of faith to pray and give serve as a constant reminder, or memorial, that we are pressing in to activate the riches of God.

Cornelius had built something before God. His prayers and giving became the vehicle God used to open His redemption to the Gentile world. Until that time the Gospel had not been spread to the Gentile population. The apostles had accepted God's redemption as being only for His chosen people, Israel.

Through his giving and praying, Cornelius paved the way for the Apostle Peter to come into a deeper revelation of God's redemption. As a result of this memorial Cornelius built, God gave Peter a vision. He revealed to Peter that He was no longer to be isolated from the Gentiles. He instructed Peter to take the message of salvation to them. Peter acted on the direction of the Holy Spirit, journeyed to Caesarea, and found Cornelius. For the first time the power of the Holy Spirit fell on a Gentile household.

Notice that this memorial Cornelius built not only brought salvation to the Gentiles, it brought the revelation to Peter that God was no respecter of nationality. The message of redemption was for all mankind.

If you will not grow cold and discouraged, but remain a person who gives to God and prays, God will bring you into new personal dimensions in Him. If necessary, He will even speak to another person to bring it to you.

God was looking for someone to move through. Cornelius had certain qualities that separated him from others. He was devoted to God in his giving and praying. If you will give God your money and the effort and discipline to be a person of prayer, He will pass over all the hard-hearted, self-serving people to move in your life.

Second Chronicles 16:9 says, **For the eyes of the Lord run to and fro throughout the whole earth, to shew himself strong in the behalf of them whose heart is perfect toward him.** God looks for a heart that is perfect or devoted to Him. Moffatt's translation says it this way: ". . . he exerts his power on behalf of those who are devoted to him."

God will move for you if you will, with an honest and devoted heart, reach out to Him through your prayers and giving. Begin to build your own memorial to God as you respond from your heart. The hunger for Him that stirs in your heart will do for you what it did for Cornelius: set in motion a visitation of the Holy Spirit that you will not miss. *It is not merely your intention to give and pray that brings God's move into your life. The devoted person will follow through with his intentions.*

Today, as the Holy Spirit works through His people, He is infusing a renewed inner strength, a fresh vision for His plan, and an enhanced revelation of His Word. He is speaking to the spirit of people, and they must hear and adhere to what He imparts.

The prophet Habakkuk said, **I will stand upon my watch, and set me upon the tower, and will watch to see what he will say unto me, and what I shall answer when I am reproved** (Hab. 2:1). Notice he was watching and listening for the word of the Lord.

And the answered me, and said, Write the vision, and make it plain upon tables, that he may run that readeth it.

For the vision is yet for an appointed time, but at the end it shall speak, and not lie: though it tarry, wait for it; because it will surely come, it will not tarry (vv. 2,3).

The Spirit said, "Write the vision." To write is to describe clearly. You must describe clearly the vision or revelation you have from God. Seek Him to understand what you must do to walk in what He is revealing to you.

Now notice verse 3 again from Moffatt's. "The vision has its own appointed hour, it ripens, it will flower; if it be long, then wait, for it is sure, and it will not be late."

In the time of personal visitation, the Holy Spirit speaks and breathes into you fresh vision and revelation. Those divine impartations will come to pass if you will cling to them and not cave in.

He said, . . . **though it tarry** (or delay), **wait for it.** To *wait* means "to adhere to."

Stick to what you know He has said. He goes on to say, . . . **because it will surely come, it will not tarry.** The word *tarry* is used twice, though not translated from the same word. The second time it means "to be late." The message is this: What He speaks to you may seem to be delayed, but continue to adhere and walk in it, because it will come and not be late.

It is so important to be specific within yourself concerning the things in which the Holy Spirit is directing you. Cornelius described to Peter *exactly* what God had revealed to him. It brought Peter into a deep revelation that God is no respecter of persons. Peter later described to the other apostles what both he and Cornelius had seen. The revelation went on to speak to many, and they understood a far deeper aspect of God's redemption than ever before.

The Holy Spirit wants to strengthen your position in Him — strengthening your grip on the things you have known and drawing you into things you have not yet understood. Paul prayed for the Ephesian church, "That you may have the power and be strong to apprehend and grasp . . ." (Eph. 3:18 AMP). It requires strength and power to grasp the things He is leading you in now!

Paul goes on in verse 19 to pray that you ". . . may have the richest measure of the divine Presence, and become a body wholly filled and flooded with God Himself!"

God is lifting His Body into a visitation of His presence. As you yield to that presence, you become an incarnation of His power. Let Him flood you with Himself.

2

Restoration: The Work of the Holy Spirit

The work of the Holy Spirit is to take the treasures of His wealth and bring them to the surface in your life. From the moment of the new birth, God is working within you to restore the areas of your life that have suffered from the impact of sin.

There is a beautiful illustration of the work of the Spirit in the Book of Nehemiah. This man, Nehemiah, was a vessel used of God to bring forth an important strength in God's people. His experience also gives us an example of what must take place in a person who is seeking restoration, stability, and spiritual strength. The Apostle Paul called these

Old Testament experiences *examples*. (I Cor. 10:6.)

In the opening lines of the Book of Nehemiah, the stage is set for a powerful revelation.

The words of Nehemiah the son of Hachaliah. And it came to pass in the month of Chisleu, in the twentieth year, as I was in Shushan the palace,

That Hanani, one of my brethren, came, he and certain men of Judah; and I asked them concerning the Jews that had escaped, which were left of the captivity, and concerning Jerusalem.

And they said unto me, The remnant that are left of the captivity there in the province are in great affliction and reproach: the wall of Jerusalem also is broken down, and the gates thereof are burned with fire.

Nehemiah 1:1-3

The city of Jerusalem was at a crucial time in its history. The temple had been rebuilt and worship had been restored, yet the walls of the city still lay in ruin.

In those days the walls of a city served several purposes. By surrounding the city, they helped to protect it from invasion. The high towers built upon these walls provided a place for watchmen to view the countryside. This vantage point gave them time to prepare the city to battle as an enemy approached. They could not be surprised.

The report came to Nehemiah many miles away in the palace of the Persian king that the people of Jerusalem were greatly afflicted and reproached because there were no walls around their city.

Nehemiah's heart sank as he heard the grim words of his kinsman. He wept and mourned for days. God's city was in desperate need, and Nehemiah was moved by God into action. He prayed that God would use him to change the condition of Jerusalem. Something had to be done. The ruined walls would have to be cleared away and new walls built. Jerusalem must again be a city that glorified Jehovah God!

Nehemiah stood before the king daily in the palace as cupbearer to Artaxerxes. This put him in a place of counsel to the king. He was so saddened by what he heard that he could not hide it from the king. He boldly requested time to go to Jerusalem with letters of authority and the supplies needed to rebuild the walls of his city. The king gave him all he asked for, as well as captains of the army to accompany him.

The report that came to Nehemiah described a city that was vulnerable to its enemies and embarrassed by its weak position. It was the cherished temple where the Possessor of heaven and earth dwelt, yet there were no walls to guard it. Though worship had been restored, Jerusalem remained vulnerable to attack from the enemy.

We are beginning to see a clear parallel developing. The conditions of Jerusalem in Nehemiah's day seem to be the conditions of countless Christians today. Because they have been born of the Spirit,

God has moved into their lives and made them His dwelling place. They have entered a position of acceptance with God. They are free to worship and enjoy His presence, yet they find themselves incapable of coping with the challenges that rise up against them. They cannot seem to bridge the gap to bring this restored relationship with God over into dealing with real-life problems. There is little control in their lives. Though they have become a temple and dwelling place of the Most High God, the walls of their soul remain in disarray.

The soul is truly the command center of your life. It is vital that you receive the work of the Holy Spirit to rebuild the crushed and ruined areas of your soul. As the walls of your soul are strengthened, you become less and less vulnerable to the attacks of your enemy, Satan. He will no longer plague you with the embarrassment of being beaten over and over again by the same weakness.

You are being built into a mighty city and fortress to bring glory to your King!

Nehemiah came to Jerusalem as the Holy Spirit comes to you — to build and strengthen your life. The picture which Nehemiah gives us of the Holy Spirit's work is so beautiful. Even his name brings this parallel. Nehemiah means "Jehovah comforts." Jesus told us, **And I will pray the Father, and he shall give you another Comforter, that he may abide with you for ever** (John 14:16). Jesus spoke of the Holy Spirit, our Comforter, whose ministry is to transform us into the very image of our heavenly Father.

Notice 2 Corinthians 3:18. **But we all, with open face beholding as in a glass the glory of the Lord, are changed into the same image from glory to glory, even as by the Spirit of the Lord.** The Comforter has come to develop your life and transform you into His image of strength and stability. He has come to free you from your enemy and make you a beautiful city that is secure. Security means to be free from cares, free from the fear of disaster, free from disease, and free from financial ruin.

The Spirit of God has come into your life with all of the tools necessary to create a life that is not vulnerable to every attack of your enemy. What makes you vulnerable? You, as a believer, are vulnerable when past sin keeps you weak. As a new creation, you are free from sin's dominion spiritually; however, your soul is in the process of being renewed. You have complete access to the presence of God.

Satan launches an attack against your soul using the areas that have defeated you before:

- He comes against your intellect with doubts, confusion, imaginations, and reasoning.

- He attacks your emotions with fear, lust, temper, anger, bitterness, and unforgiveness.

- He challenges your will with accusations of past failures or lack of resistance to compromise.
- He cripples your confidence in your ability to make a quality decision.

These past failures and compromises are the ruined walls of life which allow an entrance to Satan's strategies against you. Your defenses become weak. Your enemy's attack seems to rush upon you out of nowhere.

The Holy Spirit has come to lead you into all truth. He does not come to point His finger at your imperfections, but rather to point you to Jesus, to show you the beauty of God's kingdom and the power He has given you. He has come to restore control to your life.

Proverbs 25:28 says, **He that hath no rule over his own spirit is like a city that is broken down, and without walls.** The Spirit of God comes to stand with you against the weakness you have known. He desires to bring you to a place of confidence in moving with Him.

In Romans 8:26 Paul said it this way: **Likewise the Spirit also helpeth our infirmities.** The word *helpeth* comes from a Greek word that literally means "to take hold together with you against." The Spirit of God takes hold together with you against your weaknesses. He comes to strengthen you and stand with you as you allow God to build new strongholds in your life.

When Nehemiah first came to Jerusalem, he viewed its condition before anyone knew the purpose of his visit. Then he stood before the people of the city and said, **Ye see the distress that we are in . . . come, and let us build up the wall of Jerusalem, that we be no more a reproach** (Neh. 2:17). Notice he did not say, "Look at the mess you are in." He called it *the distress we are in*. He took upon himself the situation of the city, making it a personal problem.

The Holy Spirit also looks at what you face, not as an outsider, but from a standpoint of personal interest and involvement. But it is of extreme importance to note that the Holy Spirit does not build your life for you!

The people of Jerusalem responded to Nehemiah this way: **Let us rise up and build** (v. 18). Likewise, you must respond to the call of the Spirit of God and say, "Let us rise up together and build the walls of my life." As the Master Builder, He can make your life into a powerful fortress of strength!

The building of Jerusalem's wall was not without opposition. Sanballat was governor of Samaria, the neighboring nation. His accusations began with these words: **What is this thing that ye do? will ye rebel against the king?** (Neh. 2:19). He was challenging their actions as well as their motive. He was twisting their intentions by projecting his own wicked thoughts into them. He did not want Jerusalem strengthened. Sanballat offers a crystal clear portrayal of the tactics used by Satan against God's people.

Satan will make your steps toward God look ugly and self-serving. He might say, "Who do you think you are? You just want to do your own thing!" Or, "What right do you have to expect God to do that?" The undermining of your confidence begins with such abusive thoughts contaminating your mind.

Sanballat again hurled his accusations. **What do these feeble Jews? will they fortify themselves? will they sacrifice? will they make an end in a day? will they revive the stones out of the heaps of the rubbish which are burned?** (Neh. 4:2).

Satan mocks you as you allow the Holy Spirit to build your life. He reminds you of your human weakness. He magnifies your problem. He tries to convince you of the hopeless act of reclaiming the broken stones of the wall.

If you yield to the accusations and distortions of your enemy, the work of the Holy Spirit will cease. Answer your enemy as Nehemiah did Sanballat: **I am doing a great work, so that I cannot come down: why should the work cease,**

whilst I leave it, and come down to you? (Neh. 6:3).

The work of the Spirit went on as the people continued to work. Jerusalem was strengthened and her walls rebuilt. Strong and impenetrable, she would no longer be vulnerable to her enemies or embarrassed by her weakness.

The first words Nehemiah declared to Sanballat set the stage for what was to come. His words were prophetic. **The God of heaven, he will prosper us; therefore we his servents will arise and build: but ye have no portion, nor right, nor memorial, in Jerusalem** (Neh. 2:20). When these words came to pass, all would see that God was alive and ruler over His city.

These should also be your words to your enemy, Satan: "God is prospering me. I will rise up in the Holy Spirit and build! Satan, you have no portion of me. You have no right to me. There will be no memorial left of your work in my life!"

The Holy Spirit will then take those areas of instability and build His words into your mind, will, and emotions. Those words become the substance that resist the attempts of your enemy to keep you weak and ineffective.

He has no portion, no legal share or allotment, to you. He is portionless.

He has no right — no legal right — to your mind, thoughts, or emotions. You belong to God.

There are no memorials built within you to preserve the memory of his ability to destroy and dominate. God gets pleasure from taking what was once rubbish and broken-down areas of life and creating a life strong in the Spirit unto His glory.

Ecclesiastes 3:3 says there is a time to break down and a time to build up. The time to break down and remove the memories of failure and compromises of the past is *now*! The Spirit of God is at work in you. He has come to empower you and enable you to recover, restore, and reclaim every dimension of life that was stolen from you.

It is a time to build, so **rise up and build!**

3

Giving Place
to the Spirit

We have been destined by God to live in the Spirit, so we hunger for the supernatural. If we will move with Him, He will move in us.

After the Holy Spirit descended upon Jesus, He exhibited a tremendous change. The Spirit of heaven came to rest upon Him to reveal to all people the potential of how they could live in the power of the Holy Spirit. He began to teach the principles of the Kingdom of God and openly demonstrate its power.

The Spirit of God's grace was manifested in the likeness of a dove — gentle and beautiful, quiet and elegant. He moves with the tenderness of the sea breeze, yet He can manifest a strength like the force of the mightiest wind.

He has come to indwell you and to create a life of consistency. He comes to empower you and unite you with His supply of strength and supernatural ability.

In the Old Testament there are many exciting examples of the Holy Spirit's power moving. In 1 Samuel 10:6,7,9 the prophet Samuel told Saul what to expect as the Spirit moved upon him.

> And the Spirit of the Lord will come upon thee, and thou shalt prophesy with them, and shalt be turned into another man.
>
> And let it be, when these signs are come unto thee, that thou do as occasion serve thee; for God is with thee.
>
> And it was so, that when he had turned his back to go from Samuel, God gave him another heart: and all those signs came to pass that day.

Something dramatic happened that day: Saul became another man just as Samuel had prophesied. As he moved with the Holy Spirit, his heart was changed! Through the new birth we have entered a much deeper place in the Spirit than those under the Old Covenant, although we still need Him to move in us and change us.

Notice another example in Judges 12:24,25.

> And the woman bare a son, and called his name Samson: and the child grew, and the Lord blessed him.
>
> And the Spirit of the Lord began to move him at times.

Notice, the *Spirit moved him* at times. If the Holy Spirit could move Samson, He can move you! As this man of God grew, he learned to be used by the Spirit. In Judges 14:5,6 it says:

> Then went Samson down, and his father and his mother, to Timnath, and came to the vineyards of Timnath: and, behold, a young lion roared against him.
>
> And the Spirit of the Lord came mightily upon him, and he rent him as he would have rent a kid, and he had nothing in his hand.

39

Physically, Samson was no different than any other man in Israel. But he had entered a place in the Holy Spirit of breaking through natural limitations. When he was in a position of needing the power of God in his life, the Spirit came upon him in great strength. He had an ample supply from God that would make him more than equal to any demand.

When the lions of life roar against you, the Holy Spirit will respond in the same way if you are yielded to Him. His anointing will come upon you with the power, wisdom, and direction you need.

Breaking through some of the limitations in your life can come progressively. In many areas of life, change is not instant, but gradual. When you understand this to be a normal process, you will be free from the frustration of growing up in the Spirit.

First Corinthians 2:10 in *The Living Bible* says, ". . . his Spirit searches out and shows us all of God's deepest secrets." Those deep secrets are hidden *for* — not *from* — those who will seek Him. It is the Holy Spirit Who will bring insight to your spirit. He will begin to develop a thought, an idea, or an impression. The secret of success in the Kingdom of God becomes clearer and clearer when you realize that God's promises are truly yours.

Abram's experience helps us see how the Holy Spirit will bring deep change in us. God first spoke to Abram and revealed to him that he would be the father of many nations. (See Gen. 12:1-3.) Abram believed what God said about him, even though at that time he had fathered no one.

Romans 4:20,21 adds more depth to this event. It states:

> **He staggered not at the promise of God through unbelief; but was strong in faith, giving glory to God;**
>
> **And being fully persuaded that, what he had promised, he was able also to perform.**

Abram was "fully persuaded." He allowed the revelation to enter his

41

imagination. Once the promise was revealed to him, he put it on like a coat and wore it at all times. Yes, he made mistakes, so there is still hope for you and me. But even in his mistakes he did not leave behind what God had revealed to him.

God declared Abram to be the father of many nations; and in Abram's thoughts and imaginations, he was becoming all that was spoken of him. That is the next part of this progression in spiritual development. First, you must allow the promises of God's Word to influence your imagination. Then you must give liberty to the impressions of the Holy Spirit in your imaginations. Jesus said, "The lamp of the body is the eye. If your eye is unclouded, your whole body will be lighted up" (Matt. 6:22, *Twentieth Century*).

Your viewpoint begins to change as you receive revelation from the Spirit. If your spiritual sight remains focused properly, your imaginations "light up" with the thoughts of the Holy Spirit.

The transformation began in Abram as he consistently trusted in God's Word. Isaac was born — the child of promise; the child of revelation, imagination, and action. The principles are clear. God is teaching us (1) to regain what was lost to man at Adam's fall, (2) to cause His will to be done in the earth, and (3) to be transformed into His likeness and follow the headship of the Holy Spirit.

The Apostle Peter was dramatically changed as the revelation came to him that Jesus was the Christ. Jesus said to him, **Blessed art thou, Simon Barjona; for flesh and blood hath not revealed it unto thee, but my Father which is in heaven. And I say also unto thee, That thou art Peter . . .** (Matt. 16:17).

Peter's name had been Simon which comes from the Hebrew name meaning "obedient hearer." But because he heard, Jesus called him *Peter* which means "a large piece of rock." What Peter heard was revelation, and he was being transformed by that revelation into a rock.

43

When Jesus stood on the Mount of Transfiguration, there appeared with Him Moses and Elijah. Moses represented the Law; Elijah represented the prophets. But the Father spoke from the cloud and announced: **This is my beloved Son, in whom I am well pleased; hear ye him** (Matt. 17:5).

Jesus gives us a bold entrance into the presence of the Holy Spirit. No longer are we to live by the rules and regulations of the Law. The Holy Spirit has become our regulator. Jesus came with the words of forgiveness, acceptance, and righteousness. We are no longer connected to God through the Law and the prophets. Jesus was the fulfillment of all that Moses and Elijah represented. Now our link is with God Himself! If you will trust Him, you can be led by Him. You can hear from Him, and you can be changed to be more like Him.

He opened wide the door into the place of a higher level of participation with the Holy Spirit. He is now transforming us into people who will not hinder Him from moving, but will enhance His work.

In 2 Corinthians 3:18 there is a powerful statement about this transformation. *The Amplified Bible* reads: "And all of us, as with unveiled face, [because we] continue to behold [in the Word of God] as in a mirror the glory of the Lord, are constantly being transfigured into His very own image in ever increasing splendor and from one degree of glory to another; [for this comes] from the Lord [Who is] the Spirit."

God has deposited the potential of His divine nature within you. Through your desire for God's Word, the Holy Spirit begins to move you from this potential into experience. He will move you from victory to victory as this deposit emerges and comes to the forefront of your life, transforming you into His image, His splendor, and His glory. You may feel as though your progress has been limited and you have not

45

experienced the strength of the Holy Spirit, but God's Word says, **Let the weak say, I am strong** (Joel 3:10).

God has seen your weaknesses and frailties. But His strength within you is greater than your weakness. Stir up an awareness of His presence. He can accomplish great things in and through you as you yield to Him. Give place to the Holy Spirit and allow Him to cultivate these specific qualities as you move into new levels of involvement with Him.

1. Grow beyond potential into productiveness. Do not allow the desire to accomplish something in the Kingdom of God to be substituted by a mere fantasy about what you could do. Faith and fantasy are not even remotely related. Faith springs up from the spirit; fantasy issues merely from the soul. Make a strong commitment to pray, to tithe, and to grow in God's Word. Only then can deep progress really come.

2. Put away un-Christian attitudes. You must develop a new attitude which says,

"Others may — I may not." It is too easy to justify wrong attitudes. Sometimes we see others who are older in the Lord leaving areas unchecked and "seemingly" experiencing success, but we cannot join in.

Don't criticize or condemn others because you see a wrong attitude. Simply seek a better way. The Holy Spirit recently spoke this to me: "Others are not responsible to give Me the kind of service I ask of you. Keep your eyes on Me. Don't look for the company of many others. Much of the way you shall go will be alone, except for My presence."

3. Focus your attention and heart on things above. Colossians 3:1,2 in the Phillips translation says: ". . . reach out for the highest gifts of Heaven, where Christ reigns in power. Be concerned with the heavenly things, not to the passing things of earth." The sharper our focus, the clearer our vision.

4. Open yourself to the Holy Spirit. Stir up the anointing within. Cultivate a sensitivity to the promptings of the Spirit.

5. Be strict on yourself and easy on others. The demand God makes on you must be taken seriously. You must seek to develop an intolerance in yourself for the things He hates. But you are not to make His demands for you the measuring stick for those around you. You can influence people, but you cannot control them. You are never supposed to.

God will lead you into a new dimension of walking and living in the Spirit. You will not need to struggle to enter in, only follow. Your steps will become clear before you and your path brightly illuminated as you give place to Him!

4

Facets of His Anointing

Jesus, the Branch through which divine life and power from heaven would flow, did not live in the limitations of natural men. He did not make His decisions only by information given to Him, nor did He size up people based solely upon their appearance or actions. He had access to another dimension: the dimension of the Spirit.

The prophet Isaiah looked ahead in time and saw the anointing of the Holy Spirit resting upon the Messiah of God. He spoke clearly of the facets of that anointing that would flow through Him.

And there shall come forth a rod out of the stem of Jesse, and a Branch shall grow out of his roots:

And the spirit of the Lord shall rest upon him, the spirit of wisdom and understanding, the spirit of counsel and might, the spirit of knowledge and of the fear of the Lord;

And shall make him of quick understanding in the fear of the Lord: and he shall not judge after the sight of his eyes, neither reprove after the hearing of his ears.

Isaiah 11:1-3

The Spirit of God would rest upon Jesus and move Him according to the wisdom, counsel, and knowledge of God. He would not react by what He saw or heard. It was this dimension of the anointing which Jesus came to demonstrate.

Mankind was meant to have God's counsel and might. Jesus came to make the desire for deep involvement with God a reality. His life was not limited to natural impulses or fears. He lived with no limitations, and He has paved the way to remove the limitations for all mankind.

The Apostle Paul said this of Christ: **In whom are hid all the treasures of wisdom and knowledge** (Col. 2:3). He is in you! When He came to live within you, all His treasures came, too. The hidden treasures are deposited within you.

Just as God's power and might can be stirred within you, so can His counsel. You can receive divine counsel. The Spirit of Counsel has come. His counsel is yours today!

The miracle of counsel is as supernatural as any physical miracle. Not all miracles are confined to what we can see outwardly. There are many supernatural things God will do that are not outwardly spectacular. He can move through an entire auditorium of people with a wave of the Spirit of Counsel that will bring answers and direction to individual needs. That is supernatural!

Jesus, the Branch, has brought the life and anointing to you in the form of the Holy Spirit. The facets of His anointing upon you can flow through you to make supernatural insight and power available.

In the Book of Exodus there is a powerful example of God opening Israel's eyes to His availability. Just after the Israelites had been delivered from Pharaoh's army, they went into the desert where they had no water. God led them to the waters of Marah. Let's read Exodus 15:23-25.

> And when they came to Marah, they could not drink of the waters of Marah, for they were bitter: therefore the name of it was called Marah.
>
> And the people murmured against Moses, saying, what shall we drink?
>
> And he cried unto the Lord; and the Lord shewed him a tree, which when he had cast into the waters, the waters were made sweet.

God led them to waters which could not be consumed. He did not lead them there to drink bitter water, but to change the water from bitter to sweet.

I once heard a ridiculous interpretation of this scripture. Supposedly, God led the Israelites to the bitter water, expecting them to drink it. When they drank the water, its high mineral content (which made it bitter) would cause their bodies to be cleansed of all the impurities and toxins they had received during their oppression in Egypt. Can you imagine several million people and all their livestock being cleaned out at the same time? The truth is they never touched the bitter water to their lips. They drank sweet water!

You may be faced with "bitter waters" many times in your life. Situations, problems, or tragedies will arise to challenge your walk with God. The Holy Spirit has come to provide the wisdom, counsel, or might needed to turn those waters of life from bitter to sweet!

God told Moses to take the tree and put it into the water. Moses' obedience brought a miracle, and the miracle brought a revelation: GOD DID NOT WANT THEM TO DRINK BITTER WATERS. He is a good God; and Israel needed to know that, if they would simply obey Him, He would care for them. Yet even after the great miracles God gave them, Israel would not continue to walk with God. They refused to listen to His instructions.

Psalm 81:11-16 is a window into God's heart as He was reaching out to His nation.

> But my people would not hearken to my voice; and Israel would none of me.
>
> So I gave them up unto their own hearts' lust: and they walked in their own counsels (vv. 11,12).

Israel would not heed the counsel of God. No wonder they wandered in the wilderness. Counsel came to them as it does to you. You can heed His counsel. Listen to the results Israel could have received as the Psalm continues:

> Oh that my people had hearkened unto me, and Israel had walked in my ways!
>
> I should soon have subdued their enemies, and turned my hand against their adversaries.

54

The haters of the Lord should have submitted themselves unto him: but their time should have endured for ever.

He should have fed them also with the finest of the wheat: and with honey out of the rock should I have satisfied thee (vv. 13-16).

The Moffatt translation ends verse 16 like this: ". . . with honey from the rock to their hearts' content." Their experience could have been much different. If they had learned the lesson from the bitter waters of Marah, they would have seen how to reach out for counsel and wisdom from Jehovah God.

The tree at Marah represents the Branch in your life: Jesus Christ. The anointing He has given you can be dipped into the waters of life to turn the bitter waters sweet. Bitter rejection and disappointment is turned sweet by the Spirit of understanding flooding you. The bitterness of confusion, depression, or stagnation is sweetened as His counsel washes through you. The bitter effect of weakness, sickness, or emotional weariness is changed into strongholds of God's victory when His Spirit of might empowers you. He is as sweet as He has ever been. It's you who are being changed and sweetened. You get sweeter as the days go by.

If you continue to drink the bitter waters of life, you will eventually find yourself bitter. But as you drink the sweet waters of His counsel, wisdom, and understanding, you will see victory over the works of the devil and find yourself being sweetened.

In John 15:5 Jesus made this startling statement: **I am the vine, ye are the branches.** These words paint a most beautiful picture of our relationship with Him. Through simple faith, we allow the life of God to flow through us and bring forth fruit.

It is significant that Jesus was teaching His disciples about the vine in the final moments before His arrest. The band of officers, priests, and Pharisees were joining Judas at that very moment. Jesus' ministry was coming into a vital change. He was the Branch that the prophets had spoken about. Soon He was to become the Vine to which many branches would cling. Instead of a single branch, there would be many. These branches would also become the vessels of God's anointing as He had been.

The same Spirit which was upon the Branch is now on the branches. Jesus said, **I am the vine, ye are branches: He that abideth in me, and I in him, the same bringeth forth much fruit: for without me ye can do nothing** (John 15:5). You are in Him, abiding in Him. You can bring forth the fruit of His anointing. To *abide* means "to wait expectantly, watching for and standing ready for something; to remain stable or constant in a relationship."

To vacillate constantly — on, then off; up, then down — is not abiding. When you abide, you continue to seek God whether times are difficult or easy.

In John 15:6 comes Jesus' warning to those who will not abide in Him. **If a man**

abide not in me, he is cast forth as a branch, and is withered; and men gather them, and cast them into the fire, and they are burned.

When you cease to remain in a constant relationship with Him, you begin to wither. You actually cast yourself away from His flow of life. When situations or weaknesses influence you more than God, you will be "burned." People can burn you. Circumstances can burn you. Life can burn you.

Many people in the Kingdom of God have been burned because they would not give attention to the areas where they were not abiding. The flow of God's life was cut off from them. Their point of view was changed. They were burned by what they saw or heard. They became fruitless and useless.

A simple but profound key to stability is: keep your eyes focused on Jesus, not on others.

Then in John 15:7,8 comes Jesus' tremendous promise and pathway of discipleship. The Wuest translation is so descriptive. It reads: "If you maintain a living communion with me and my words are at home in you, I command you to ask, at once, something for yourself, whatever your heart desires, and it will become yours. In this my Father is glorified, namely, that you are bearing much fruit. So shall you become my disciples."

Fruitfulness in life is possible only by a continued living relationship in the Holy Spirit. Deep communion comes out of your union with Him. The strength of redemption is released through this deep relationship.

You can begin to stir up the various facets of God's anointing and know the direction He is leading you. His desires will become clearer in you. They will become your desires as a result of your closeness with Him. They are not desires of your flesh or mind. They spring up from within your heart. You can know what God is speaking to you by giving attention to the desires of your heart.

God speaks in many ways. He speaks through visions and dreams, through His prophets and ministers, through His written Word, even audibly at times. He speaks Spirit to spirit, and He speaks through desires.

He places a desire within your heart, then He inspires you to ask for it. In that way, He can give you whatever your heart desires. He has initiated it. A disciple who brings glory to the Father God is one who is following the leading of the Holy Spirit. He seeks to do those things which please God. He listens for the counsel and knowledge of the Spirit that he may express the anointing.

The Holy Spirit is pulling and lifting you into an active involvement with Him. His wisdom, His counsel, and His might will wash through you so you can flow with Him and bear much fruit.

5

Yielding to the Holy Spirit

We are living in the age of the Holy Spirit. At the end of His ministry, Jesus said He would send the Holy Spirit to lead us into the truth that He came to reveal.

In John 7:38 Jesus was speaking of the Holy Spirit when He said, **He that believeth on me, as the scripture hath said, out of his belly shall flow rivers of living water.**

The Holy Spirit has come and is releasing life-giving waters that lie deep within the one who will yield to Him. The Holy Spirit opens your eyes to see life from His perspective. The one who is yielded to the Holy Spirit will find

61

himself taking on new interests and priorities in life.

Fruitfulness in life comes as a result of yielding to the Spirit. To *yield* means "to give up or to give yourself over." It is also "to open yourself with an open hand to receive from another."

Yielding to the Holy Spirit means that you give up your own ideas and efforts, and put yourself in His hand. You approach Him with an empty hand that is open and ready to receive from Him. It is impossible to grasp one thing when your hand is holding onto something else.

There are different levels of relationship with the Holy Spirit which are important to understand. The first relationship we will discuss is the Spirit with us. The fact that He is in the earth today gives every person the potential of a personal relationship with Him. There is no one He cannot reach and no one who cannot reach Him. He is available to all, but His availability does not mean there is automatically a relationship with Him.

In John 14:16,17 Jesus said:

And I will pray the Father, and he shall give you another Comforter, that he may abide with you for ever;

Even the Spirit of truth; whom the world cannot receive, because it seeth him not, neither knoweth him: but ye know him: for he dwelleth with you, and shall be in you.

The disciples witnessed the influence of the Holy Spirit among them. However, they had not yet moved from an outer experience of His presence to His indwelling. They knew Him outwardly, but soon He would come to dwell within them.

This brings us to the second type of relationship we can experience with the Holy Spirit: His indwelling. The prophet Ezekiel spoke of this relationship.

Then will I sprinkle clean water upon you, and ye shall be clean: from all your filthiness, and from all your idols, will I cleanse you.

A new heart also will I give you, and a new spirit will I put within you: and I will take away the stony heart

out of your flesh, and I will give you an heart of flesh.

And I will put my spirit within you, and cause you to walk in my statutes, and ye shall keep my judgments, and do them.

Ezekiel 36:25-27

The desire of the Holy Spirit as described in Ezekiel was to make man His dwelling place. He would remove the stony heart and replace it with a heart that is tender and sensitive toward Himself. This tenderhearted man would be alive to the Spirit, able to commune with God and enjoy His presence.

The third level of our relationship with the Holy Spirit is found in the book of Acts. "But you shall receive power — ability, efficiency and might — when the Holy Spirit has come upon you" (Acts 1:8 AMP).

Jesus said the Holy Spirit would come upon you. As you yield to Him, His power increases as it moves through you. His ability, His efficiency, and His might all become yours. You are yielding and surrendering to Him.

The Holy Spirit begins to reveal His presence to you. He develops the fruit of the Spirit within you, making you fruitful. He creates a sensitivity to His impulses, and as a result you rise to new dimensions of His power.

The life you lived before you received Christ was governed by the appetites and impulses of the carnal nature. If your flesh wanted it, it got it! Life was nearly consumed with catering to anything your flesh desired. Christians who continue to pamper their flesh will never become strong. They will never be satisfied within because they cannot please God. Deep within them is the desire to please Him, but unchanged they remain of little use or effectiveness to the work of the Holy Spirit.

There are those, however, who are unsatisfied with carnal life so they reach out for something more. They want to be sensitive and useful to the Holy Spirit. They want to be "a vessel for honor, sanctified, useful to the Master, prepared for every good work" (2 Tim. 2:21 NAS).

Let's read what the Apostle Paul wrote in Romans 8:5,9 from *The Amplified Bible:*

"But those who are according to the Spirit and [controlled by the desires] of the Spirit, set their minds on and seek those things which gratify the (Holy) Spirit.

"But you are not living the life of the flesh, you are living the life of the Spirit, if the (Holy) Spirit of God [really] dwells within you — directs and controls you."

Paul addressed the Ephesians this way:

And be renewed in the spirit of your mind;

And that ye put on the new man, which after God is created in righteousness and true holiness.

Ephesians 4:23,24

To more fully cooperate with the Holy Spirit, you must refuse to yield to the distractions that Satan uses to draw you back. Yielding to the Spirit means to give your thoughts and imaginations over to Him. You must think the thoughts of the Spirit. Instead of thinking destructive ideas that are negative — full of defeat and despair — yield to the ideas of the Holy Spirit. Let Him bring power into your life through the Word of God.

Proverbs 16:3 AMP says, "Roll your works upon the Lord — commit and trust them wholly to Him; [He will cause your thoughts to become agreeable to His will, and] so shall your plans be established and succeed."

As you roll your works upon the Lord, the Holy Spirit causes your thoughts to become an expression of His will. By yielding to God's will, you are being molded by His influence into the likeness of Jesus. He truly begins to take control. Some people are controlled by their flesh, others are under the influence of demon spirits. You are being controlled and influenced by the Holy Spirit. You have become more sensitive to His sweet presence. He begins to send impulses to your heart, and you respond to His quiet leading. You find that your steps are being directed by the hand of the Spirit of God.

You are a vessel containing His presence, a vehicle transporting His power.

Not long ago you might have collapsed in the face of the challenges before you. Instead, you have silenced the promptings of carnal thinking. You are no longer moved by outer pressure. You look to the Holy Spirit as He brings the Word of God to life. You stand strong in His strength. "I have strength for all things in Christ Who empowers me — I am ready for anything and equal to anything through Him Who infuses inner strength into me, [that is, I am self-sufficient in Christ's sufficiency]" (Phil. 4:13 AMP).

You are walking in and with the Holy Spirit. It is a continuous attitude of the heart to reach out for the things of the Spirit — step by step, actively yielding to His influence. You take on the appearance of one who knows where he is going and what he is doing. You are self-sufficient in Christ's sufficiency.

Many voices may come to advise you on what steps to take, but you simply filter them out. You know the voice of the Master. When you know Him, you can pick His voice out of the crowd. You can sense His leading and direction. Peace comes over you as you follow His course of action. If you begin to stray off course, an uneasiness seems to shout, STOP! as though it were a flashing red light.

God's Word has become a living lamp to your feet. Your walk with Him becomes more intimate. Your path becomes narrow, your steps more sure.

This yielded walk is emphasized many places in the Epistles. In Galatians, Paul says, **This I say then, Walk in the Spirit, and ye shall not fulfil the lust of the flesh** (Gal. 5:16). Again in the same book, he says, **If we live in the Spirit, let us also walk in the Spirit** (Gal. 5:25). The word *walk* gives us this idea: "Be constantly conducting yourself in the Spirit."

In Ephesians, he says, **I therefore, the prisoner of the Lord, beseech you that ye walk worthy of the vocation wherewith ye are called** (Eph. 4:1). Later he says,

Walk not as other Gentiles walk . . . walk in love . . . walk as children of light . . . walk circumspectly (Eph. 4:17; 5:2,8,15).

In Colossians, he says, **As ye have therefore received Christ Jesus the Lord, so walk ye in him** (Col. 2:6).

In Thessalonians, he says, **. . . as ye have received of us how ye ought to walk and to please God, so ye would abound more and more** (1 Thess. 4:1).

Then in 1 John, we are told clearly by the Spirit to walk even as He walks for as He is, so are we in this world. (1 John 2:6; 4:17).

These statements would overwhelm anyone unless they could see just how Jesus walked. Notice in Luke 4:1,14 from *The Amplified Bible:* "Then Jesus, full of and controlled by the Holy Spirit, returned from the Jordan, and was led in (by) the (Holy) Spirit . . . Then Jesus went back full of and under the power of the (Holy) Spirit into Galilee, and the fame of Him spread through the whole region round about."

He was full of and controlled by the Holy Spirit! That will be said of you when you walk in the Spirit. Jesus was born of the Holy Spirit, free from the dominion of sin. Through simple faith in Jesus' sacrifice, you have been born of the same Spirit and made free from the dominion of sin. In the same manner that Jesus was under the direction of the Holy Spirit, you also are under His influence. As you yield to Him, He will direct your steps.

Jesus spoke with boldness as He announced God's willingness to deliver and heal people. When the religious people in the synagogue first heard Him speak, they were enraged by His familiarity with Jehovah God because He revealed their hardness of heart. They were so angry that they rose up to silence Him. They took Him to the edge of a cliff to cast Him to His death, but Jesus would not be pushed! He passed through the mob, and they were powerless to stop Him.

Why was He in control? Why were those demon-inspired people unable to destroy Him? Because He was full of and controlled by the Holy Spirit. Your enemy cannot control you and push you over a cliff. You may feel on the edge of losing control completely, but God is ready to refresh you and restore your control. Reach out to Him now.

When Israel was wandering through the wilderness, they were given a cloud by day and a pillar of fire by night. When the cloud began to move, there could be no argument: they had to pack their belongings and move with it.

The Spirit leads, He never follows! If you begin to lead, you walk alone. If you fight the moving of the Holy Spirit in your life, you may discover yourself out from under the cloud and alone in the scorching heat of the desert.

One very real hindrance in yielding to the influence of the Holy Spirit is one of Satan's most effective weapons: false condemnation. He reminds you of your past pride, worldliness, or fruitlessness. Than he fills you with a fear of future failures.

Despair and depression may draw you into a tailspin as you let your thoughts run rampant.

Satan will say to you, "Look at yourself. You call yourself a Christian! Do you think you could really be led by the Holy Spirit? With all of the problems and defeats you have had, you would be a fool to think your future can be any different."

The difference between Satan's condemnation and the Holy Spirit's conviction is that Satan points to the past or the future. But the Spirit of God points you to the image of Christ and deals specifically with the present. God sees your past through the eyes of forgiveness and your future through the eyes of hope. He sees you in Christ. He does not want you to focus your sight on past weakness, but upon your present ability in the power of the Holy Spirit.

He is now doing what Jesus promised He would do: bringing to light the ability of the Father and the Son, and building it into your life. He is opening the Word and making it alive.

The Spirit of Heaven is the Spirit of Creation, the Spirit of the Resurrection, and the Spirit Life. He has come to guide, direct, empower, and energize you. Yield to Him!

"In conclusion, be strong in the Lord — be empowered through your union with Him; draw your strength from Him — that strength which His [boundless] might provides" (Eph. 6:10 AMP).

References

New American Standard Bible (NAS). Copyright © The Lockman Foundation 1960, 1962, 1963, 1968, 1971, 1973, 1975, 1977, La Habra, California.

The Amplified Bible, New Testament (AMP). Copyright © 1954, 1958 by The Lockman Foundation, La Habra, California.

The Amplified Bible, Old Testament (AMP). Copyright © 1962, 1964 by Zondervan Publishing House, Grand Rapids, Michigan.

The Bible: A New Translation (Mof). Copyright © 1950, 1952, 1953, 1954 by James A. R. Moffatt. Harper & Row, Publishers, Inc., New York, New York.

The Living Bible (TLB). Copyright © 1971 by Tyndale House Publishers, Wheaton, Illinois.

NOTES

NOTES

NOTES

NOTES